I0476495

STEP BY STEP GUIDE TO HELP YOU THROUGH A JOB INTERVIEW

Purpose of an Interview

The main purpose of a job interview is to provide an opportunity for an employer and a job candidate to meet to determine if a mutual fit exists between the candidate's skills and experience and the organization's needs.

As a job candidate, you should use a job interview to:

- Showcase your skills and qualifications in connection with the position
- Demonstrate your enthusiasm for the job and a strong fit with the company
- Determine whether or not this position suits your career goals and objectives
- Evaluate how well the corporate culture matches your values and interests

When You are Invited to Interview:

- Clarify who you will be meeting with
- Ask about length of interview
- Obtain a full job description, if available
- Inquire whether any company handout information is available
- Write down the date and time of the interview
- Obtain location of interview and directions, if necessary
- Ask if any technical testing will take place

How to Prepare for an Interview:

- Conduct further research on the company and develop a clear understanding of how you fit with the organization
- Know and understand the job description
- Identify your key skills, strengths and characteristics that relate to the job
- Review your resume to be familiar with all of your experiences that relate to the job
- Practice answering interview questions as they relate to the job description
- Prepare your own questions to ask the interviewer

What to Bring to an Interview:

- Portfolio to carry all of your papers
- Copy of your resume
- Official transcript
- List of references
- Copies of any relevant projects or reports
- List of 3 or 4 questions to ask at the end of the interview
- Pen and extra paper in case you need to make notes during the interview

When Interviewing for a Job, Remember to:

- Stay focused on why you should be chosen for the job
- Know why you are a good candidate (i.e. know your strengths and values)
- Be able to identify your skills and be prepared to offer examples of where you developed them

How to Make a Positive Impression During an Interview:

- Pay attention to your personal grooming (hair combed; nails trimmed; clean appearance ; ironed clothes)
- Wear professional attire (business suit, dress shirt, matching shoes)
- Maintain eye contact
- Be aware of and control your non-verbal behaviour
- Bring extra copies of your resume and a copy of your transcript
- Plan to arrive 15 minutes early
- Offer a firm handshake
- Answer questions concisely and directly
- Avoid insincere flattery, bravado and cockiness
- Present yourself in a positive & professional manner
- Let your enthusiasm for the position shine through

Useful Tips for Answering Interview Questions:

- Never volunteer any negative information to the employer, unless specifically requested to do so then include what you learned or gained from the experience
- Be able to provide concrete examples of your skills from your educational, work or extracurricular experiences
- Try to read between the lines - think about what is really being asked
- If you don't understand the question, ask for further clarification
- If you need a minute to think about your answer, request this of the interviewer to avoid any awkward silences
- Know yourself - your strengths and values

- If you are interviewing with more than one person, be sure to include all interviewers when answering questions by making eye contact with everyone
- Understand the theory behind behaviour based interview questions

Standard Format for an Interview

Although the length may vary, most interviews follow four standard stages:

1. Greetings & Introductions

- Introduce yourself and shake hands with each interviewer
- Interviewer's goal is to utilize small talk to make you feel comfortable, calm and more relaxed in an effort to prepare you for the next part of the interview
- Your goal is to make a strong first impression with your manners, body language and smile
- Allow the interviewer to guide you on when and where to take a seat

2. Question & Answer Period

- Interviewer may begin with a brief description of the job responsibilities and the organization's plans with respect to the position
- Prior to beginning with their list of questions, an interviewer may begin with a general request for you to tell them a little bit more about yourself (give a brief one minute overview of your background and be sure to connect this closely with their company and the job you are applying)
- Interviewer will ask you questions to determine whether or not you can do the job and how you will fit into the organization
- Through this process, interviewers are also testing your communication and interpersonal skills
- Your goal is to answer all questions effectively to clearly demonstrate your fit with the position
- Listen closely to what the interviewer is asking you to ensure that you eliminate any doubts they may have about your suitability for this job

3. Opportunity for You to Ask the Interviewer a Few Questions

- Have 3 or 4 questions prepared to ask the interviewer that demonstrate your understanding of the position and the company
- Ask questions about potential projects, training, supervision, performance evaluation and corporate goals
- Use your questions to highlight the skills that make you suitable for this position
- You can also use your questions to demonstrate the amount of research you have done on their company
- Do not ask any questions during the interview that appear self-serving, such as "What will my salary be?" or "Can I have 2 week vacation in July?"
- Questions about salary and vacation can be asked at the time a job offer is extended, but they are not appropriate for a job interview

4. Wrap Up

- Interviewer may use the last few minutes of the interview to discuss what happens next, such as timelines for hiring or future interview dates
- Offer your list of references if the employer doesn't request it
- Your goal is to demonstrate your enthusiasm for the position and express interest in their company
- Thank the interviewer for meeting with you and shake hands
- If you are interested in the position, ask the employer for a business card

Three mistakes people make during an interview

Not enough confidence – For any job, any field, any industry one thing that an employer wants you to have is confidence. Having confidence does not mean walking into an interview acting like you already have the job and like you own the place. It simply means believing in yourself, your knowledge and your abilities. What you want to get across to the interviewer is that you can do the job. If you think about it there are two reasons that employers want to get out of an interview. Number 1 – Can you do the job? , Number 2 – Will you fit in with the rest of the team? If you can convince the employer of these two things you're in. When someone is lacking confidence and they are being interviewed it creates other problems that originally were not there, things such as being nervous, losing your train of thought and not giving the complete answer. When applying for a position you should know that you can do the job otherwise you will be setting yourself up for failure. This is the case with a lot of people but we'll leave this for another discussion. So, if you're already at the interview stage it means that you have passed the pre-screening process and that the employer obviously liked what they have seen regarding your education and experience which means that you have no reason not to be confident. Many people do not realize that getting the interview is a very big deal and should try not to be nervous and basically should just concentrate on expressing everything that they have on their resumes verbally. This should not be hard if you are really familiar with your resume and if you can think of really good examples of your past work experiences.

Too much confidence – I'll start off be repeating what I said under the first point "Having confidence does not mean walking into an interview acting like you already have the job and like you own the place. It simply means believing in yourself, your knowledge and your abilities.". Very large numbers of people believe that they are simply the best and that no one else compares to them, this most likely is NOT the case. People with too much confidence come across as being stubborn and usually are not liked by the employers because it makes the employer believe that if you are hired you will refuse certain jobs because you might think that you are above certain things and that you only deserve to do jobs that are considered to be high level. People that fall in this category are often thought of as not being team players and that they will be high maintenance employees because their expectations will be very high. This is something you do not want to do in an interview. Be confident but do not take it too far.

Not knowing enough about the position or the company – This might not make a lot of sense to people that are very organized in their job search and to those that keep track of every position that they apply to but it happens more than people realize. This is the one mistake that can be fixed without much effort; all it takes is some organization. Individuals that apply to a large number of positions often forget where they have applied, if they have sent an email, applied on-line through the company's website or if they simply gave their resume to a friend. Keeping track of your applications is very important. This is the reason a lot of people get confused about the specifics of a certain position and forget to do their research on the company. Employers love it when an applicant comes in and is able to discuss the specifics of a position and also to be able to talk about the direction their company is headed in. It is always a good idea to come to the interview with a few questions which ask about the position and the team that you would be working with as well as the growth possibility of the company and some of the major contracts that they are currently working on. Questions like this show the interviewer that you are genuinely interested in the position and the company since you have done a lot of research and are familiar with their work.

What to Do After the Interview

Finally, the interview is over and you have done everything you can to secure a job offer from that employer, right? Wrong, here are some tips on what to do after you leave the interview room:

- Immediately following the interview, write down the interviewer's name (if you didn't obtain a business card) and your thoughts about the company and position – if you are interviewing for numerous jobs over a period of time, this technique will help you keep all of your job applications straight and provide you with a pro/con list if a job offer is extended
- Send a Thank You note/email to the interviewer
- If the employer falls behind on the hiring timeline that was discussed with you during the interview, follow up with a phone call to inquire about the status of the position
- If you do not get the job, ask for some feedback from the employer so that you can be better prepared for the next job interview you obtain

Interview Do's & Don'ts:

- Do maintain a positive, professional attitude
- Do answer questions clearly and thoroughly – if you are unsure whether or not you have provided enough information, ask the employer if they require further clarification
- Do demonstrate enthusiasm for the company, industry and position
- Do conduct extensive research on the company and the industry before the interview
- Do practice answering questions prior to the interview
- Do prepare some questions in advance that you would like to ask the interviewer
- Do maintain eye contact

- Don't refer negatively to past employers or jobs – if an interviewer asks you share a negative experience, place emphasis on how you handled the situation and what you learned from it to develop effective coping mechanisms in the future
- Don't arrive late for an interview – plan to arrive at least 15 minutes early
- Don't talk in generalities – be specific about your skills and use concrete examples to back up your points
- Don't slouch or sit with your arms firmly crossed - be aware of your body language and the unconscious messages you may be sending
- Don't act chummy with the interviewer or tell jokes – instead, maintain a friendly, professional attitude
- Don't dress casually for a job interview – make sure that your outfit is business-like so that you convey a professional image. Don't forget about your shoes – running shoes does not go with a suit!

Types of Interview Questions

In interviews that are considered to be structured there are typically two types of questions interviewers will use: behavioural questions and situational questions. Both types of questions are based on critical incidents that are required to perform the job but they differ in their focus.

Analyses have found mixed results for which type of question will best predict future job performance of an applicant. For example, some studies have shown that situational type questions have better predictability for job performance in interviews, while, other researchers have found that behavioral type questions are better at predicting future job performance of applicants. In actual interview settings it is not likely that the sole use of just one type of interview question is asked. A range of questions can add variety for both the interviewer and applicant. In addition, the use of high-quality questions, whether behavioral or situational based, is essential to make sure that candidates provide meaningful responses that lead to insight into their capability to perform on the job.

Behaviour Based Interviewing:

Behaviour based interviewing is a technique used by employers to learn about how you have behaved in past experiences in order to better predict how you will perform in their job. When answering this type of interview question, it is very important to refer to a specific situation and talk about what you did and how it turned out.

It is imperative that you practice for this type of interview, to allow yourself to become comfortable speaking about your past experiences as they relate to this job. How to prepare for a behaviour based interview:

- Review the job description and highlight the skills required to perform effectively in this position
- For each skill required, think about 2 or 3 examples from your past educational, work or extra-curricular experiences of when you have demonstrated this skill
- Practice speaking about each related experience – remember to explain:

- The situation in which you demonstrated the skill
- The challenges you faced in association with this experience
- The actions you took in this situation
- The end result or outcome of the experience

Sample Behaviour Based Questions:

- Describe a situation when you were able to identify a conflict between two individuals and were instrumental in the solution to that conflict.
- How do you behave when you encounter a problem with a co-worker?
- Tell us about a time when you experienced a steep learning curve in a job. What did you do to learn all the material you needed to know?
- How do you decide what gets top priority when scheduling your time?

Example of How to Answer Behaviour Based Question:

Sample Question –

Please describe a time when you were working within a team and you experienced difficulties meeting the project deadline due to communication problems. How did you handle this problem?

Sample Response –

During my internship with ABC Company, I was working with a team of 5 individuals to evaluate 3 new software packages to determine the best replacement for the current assembly line computer system (Situation). We were supposed to meet weekly to review each package and discuss our concerns, but each week one or two of the team members were away on holidays and we were continually canceling meetings. Because each person represented the interests of a different department, no consensus could be reached unless all of the group members were present. We needed adequate time to review each new package, but we were faced with a deadline date less than 2 weeks away to reach a decision about the best new product so that the package could be purchased and put into place by October 1st (Challenges). To resolve the problem, I contacted each group member to obtain their holiday schedule over the next two weeks. After reviewing the schedules, I suggested 5 possible times we could meet over the next two weeks in order to meet our deadline date. From their feedback regarding these days, I arranged 3 meeting times to discuss each of the packages and asked that if a member was unable to attend, they send a representative from their department in their place (Actions). We met as scheduled on all three occasions, and only one member missed one meeting due to an emergency with their daughter, but their replacement fit in well and offered some valuable input to the group. Our deadline was reached 2 days ahead of schedule and the new software was in place by September 21st. From this experience, I learned the importance of communicating as a group and finding creative solutions when the group is faced with scheduling challenges (Result).

Situational interview questions

Situational interview questions ask job applicants to imagine a set of conditions and then specify how they would respond in that situation; hence, the questions are future oriented. One advantage of situational questions is that all interviewees respond to the same hypothetical situation rather than describe experiences unique to them from their past. Another advantage is that situational questions allow respondents who have had no direct job experience relevant to a particular question to provide a hypothetical response. Two core aspects of the SI are the development of situational dilemmas that employees encounter on the job, and a scoring guide to evaluate responses to each dilemma.

Situational examples

- You are in charge of truck drivers in Toronto. Your colleague is in charge of truck drivers in Montreal. Both of you report to the same person. Your salary and bonus are affected 100% by your costs. Your colleague is in desperate need of one of your trucks. If you say no, your costs will remain low and your group will probably win the Golden Flyer award for the quarter. If you say yes, the Montreal group will probably win this prestigious award because they will make a significant profit for the company. Your boss is preaching costs, costs, costs, as well as co-operation with one's peers. Your boss has no control over accounting who are the score keepers. Your boss is highly competitive; he or she rewards winners. You are just as competitive; you are a real winner! What would you do in this situation?

- You are in a meeting. Your manager blames you for not doing well on a task, in front of all your peers and managers from other divisions. You believe that your manager is wrong in his critique, and that he might have come to this conclusion hastily without knowing all the information. You feel you are being treated unfairly in front of your peers. You feel that your reputation may be affected by this critique. What would you do in this situation?

- You are managing a work group and notice that one of your employees has become angry and hostile in recent weeks, to the point of disrupting the entire group. What would you do?

- A general request has been issued by the Dean for someone to serve on a new joint government/industry/university committee on business education. The objective of the committee is to design the budgeting allocation for the Faculty for the next fiscal year. It is well known that you have the necessary skill and expertise to improve the chances that the Faculty will receive budget increases for future operations. You have been told that it will require 2–3 days per month of your time for the next 9 months. Your tenure review is one year away. Although you think you have a good publication record, you have no guarantee of tenure at this point. You are concerned because you have already fallen behind on an important research project that you are pursuing with a colleague at another university. What, if anything, would you do?

Other types of questions

Other possible types of questions that may be asked in an interview include: background questions, job experience questions, and puzzle type questions. A brief explanation of each follows.

Background questions include a focus on work experience, education, and other qualifications. For instance, an interviewer may ask "What experience have you had with direct sales phone calls?"

Job experience questions may ask candidates to describe or demonstrate job knowledge. These are typically highly specific questions. For example, one question may be "What steps would you take to conduct a manager training session on safety?"

The puzzle interview was popularized by Microsoft in the 1990s, and is now used in other organizations. The most common types of questions either ask the applicant to solve puzzles or brain teasers (e.g., "Why are manhole covers round?") or to solve unusual problems (e.g., "How would you weigh an airplane without a scale?").

Case

A case interview is an interview form used mostly by management consulting firms and investment banks in which the job applicant is given a question, situation, problem or challenge and asked to resolve the situation. The case problem is often a business situation or a business case that the interviewer has worked on in real life. In recent years, company in other sectors like Design, Architecture, Marketing, Advertising, Finance and Strategy have adopted a similar approach to interviewing candidates. Technology has transformed the Case based and Technical interview process from a purely private in-person experience to an online exchange of job skills and endorsements.

Panel

Another type of job interview found throughout the professional and academic ranks is the panel interview. In this type of interview the candidate is interviewed by a group of panelists representing the various stakeholders in the hiring process. Within this format there are several approaches to conducting the interview. Example formats include;

Presentation format – The candidate is given a generic topic and asked to make a presentation to the panel. Often used in academic or sales-related interviews.

Role format – Each panelist is tasked with asking questions related to a specific role of the position. For example one panelist may ask technical questions, another may ask management questions, another may ask customer service related questions etc.

Skeet shoot format – The candidate is given questions from a series of panelists in rapid succession to test his or her ability to handle stress filled situations.

The benefits of the panel approach to interviewing include: time savings over serial interviewing, more focused interviews as there is often less time spend building rapport with small talk, and "apples to apples" comparison because each stake holder/interviewer/panelist gets to hear the answers to the same questions.

Stress

Stress interviews are still in common use. One type of stress interview is where the employer uses a succession of interviewers (one at a time or en masse) whose mission is to intimidate the candidate and keep him/her off-balance. The ostensible purpose of this interview: to find out how the candidate handles stress. Stress interviews might involve testing an applicant's behavior in a busy environment. Questions about handling work overload, dealing with multiple projects, and handling conflict are typical.

Another type of stress interview may involve only a single interviewer who behaves in an uninterested or hostile manner. For example, the interviewer may not make eye contact, may roll his eyes or sigh at the candidate's answers, interrupt, turn his back, take phone calls during the interview, or ask questions in a demeaning or challenging style. The goal is to assess how the interviewee handles pressure or to purposely evoke emotional responses. This technique was also used in research protocols studying stress and type A (coronary-prone) behavior because it would evoke hostility and even changes in blood pressure and heart rate in study subjects. The key to success for the candidate is to de-personalize the process. The interviewer is acting a role, deliberately and calculatedly trying to "rattle the cage". Once the candidate realizes that there is nothing personal behind the interviewer's approach, it is easier to handle the questions with aplomb.

Example stress interview questions:

- Sticky situation: "If you caught a colleague cheating on his expenses, what would you do?"
- Putting you on the spot: "How do you feel this interview is going?"
- Popping the balloon: (deep sigh) "Well, if that's the best answer you can give ... " (shakes head) "Okay, what about this one ...?"
- Oddball question: "What would you change about the design of the hockey stick?"
- Doubting your veracity: "I don't feel like we're getting to the heart of the matter here. Start again – tell me what really makes you tick."

Candidates may also be asked to deliver a presentation as part of the selection process. The "Platform Test" method involves having the candidate make a presentation to both the selection panel and other candidates for the same job. This is obviously highly stressful and is therefore useful as a predictor of how the candidate will perform under similar circumstances on the job. Selection processes in academic, training, airline, legal and teaching circles frequently involve presentations of this sort.

Technical

This kind of interview focuses on problem solving and creativity. The questions aim at the interviewee's problem-solving skills and likely show their ability in solving the challenges faced in the job through creativity. Technical interviews are being conducted online at progressive companies before in-person talks as a way to screen job applicants.

Telephone

Telephone interviews take place if a recruiter wishes to reduce the number of prospective candidates before deciding on a shortlist for face-to-face interviews. They also take place if a job applicant is a significant distance away from the premises of the hiring company, such as abroad or in another state or province.

Video

Video interviews are a modern variation of telephone interviews. Prospective candidates are asked preset questions using computer software then their immediate responses are recorded. These responses are then viewed and evaluated by recruiters to form a shortlist of suitable candidates for face-to-face interviews

Practice Interview Questions

Listed below are some common questions asked by employers during job interviews. Read these questions over carefully and practice responses you would give during an actual interview. Prior to your job interviews, you may find it helpful to practice your answers with your family or friends.

The questions provided below are meant to serve only as a guideline to help you prepare for the interview. Some questions may or may not be appropriate for your interviewing situation.

CAREER GOALS

1. What are your long range career goals? Short range goals?

2. What specific goals, other than those related to your career, have you established?

3. Please describe the accomplishments you have achieved in your career so far.

4. How does this assignment fit into your overall career plan?

5. What are the most important rewards you expect in your career?

6. Why did you choose the career for which you are preparing?

7. How would you describe your ideal job following graduation?

8. What qualifications do you have that make you think you will be successful in your career?

9. How do you define "success?"

10. Where do you see yourself in 5 years?

GENERAL SKILLS/ATTRIBUTES

1. Tell me about yourself. (try to hold your response to 2-3 minutes)

2. Describe a time when you prepared and communicated ideas and information in a formal setting.

3. If a friend or professor were asked to describe you, what would he/she say?

4. What do you consider to be your greatest strengths and weaknesses?

5. What motivates you to put forth your greatest effort?

6. What have you learned from your mistakes?

7. Tell me about three of your accomplishments of which you are the most proud.

8. Identify a major problem you've encountered and how you dealt with it.

9. Can you tell me about how you make important decisions?

10. What personal attributes do you feel are necessary to succeed in this field?

WORK SPECIFIC SKILLS/ATTRIBUTES

1. Describe your ideal job.

2. Describe your management philosophy.

3. What were the three most significant accomplishments in your last job?

4. What have you learned from some of the jobs you have held?

5. What specific things did you do in your last job to improve your effectiveness?

6. What did you like least and most about your last job? What did you learn?

7. Can you work well under deadlines or pressure?

8. Describe what types of software packages you feel comfortable using.

9. Describe a situation when you were able to identify a conflict between two individuals and were instrumental in the solution to that conflict.

10. How would your colleagues (or your boss) describe you?

EDUCATION

1. Why did you select your University?

2. How is university preparing you for your career?

3. Tell me more about your program.

4. Why did you choose your major field of study?

5. What courses do you like the best? The least? Why?

6. Do you think your grades are an accurate indication of your academic achievement?

7. How do you think your academic performance will influence your ability to perform well in this job?

8. What areas do you perceive a need for additional training in this position?

9. What extra-curricular activities have you been involved with at your university or in your community?

10. What have you learned from participation in extra-curricular activities?

KNOWLEDGE OF JOB

1. In your opinion, what skills and qualifications are essential to be successful in this position?

2. What do you find satisfying about this kind of work?

3. What interests you most about this job opportunity? Least?

4. What can you offer us that someone else cannot?

5. Why should we hire you?

6. What preparation have you had for this position?

7. If you took the job, what would you accomplish in the first 6 months?

8. How long do you think it would take you to make a positive contribution to our organization?

9. In this position, the ability to function well within a team environment would be important. Describe a situation where your participated in a team to complete a project.

10. Describe any previous experience you have had that would help contribute to your success in this position.

KNOWLEDGE OF COMPANY

1. What do you know about our company?

2. Why do you want to work for us?

3. What impresses you most about our organization?

4. What have you heard about our company that you don't like?

5. Our company is much larger (smaller) than the previous companies you have worked for. How do you feel about that?

6. What criteria have you used to evaluate the companies that you hope to do a work placement with?

7. How does our company compare with your previous employer(s)?

8. How would you contribute to the overall goals of the company?

9. How will you make a difference in our company?

10. How familiar are you with our organization?

WORK ENVIRONMENT

1. What kind of supervisor or boss do you prefer?

2. Describe the relationship that should exist between a supervisor and subordinates.

3. What types of people seem to "rub you the wrong way?"

4. Do you prefer working with others or by yourself?

5. How do you behave when you encounter a problem with a co-worker?

6. Describe the kind of a work environment are you are most comfortable with: structured, unstructured, etc.

7. How do you go about making important decisions?

8. Do you anticipate problems well or merely react to them?

9. Tell me about a few new procedures you have instituted in your previous jobs. How effective where they and how did your co-workers react?

10. Would you prefer a large or a small company? Why?

FINAL QUESTIONS

1. How do you spend your spare time?

2. What other positions are you considering?

3. How long would it take you to be productive in this position?

4. Which is more important to you, money or job satisfaction?

5. How do you feel about working evenings or overtime?

6. Is there anything that will prevent you from taking this job if offered?

7. Is there anything else about you I should know?

8. Do you have any questions for me?

9. Do you have your reference list with you? (Remember to offer it at the end, if they don't ask for it)

10. Do you mind if I contact your references?

Questions for the Interviewer

In addition to practicing how to answer interview questions, job candidates should prepare 3 or 4 questions to ask the employer at the end of the interview. If you don't come prepared with your own questions to ask, the interviewer may conclude that you are not very serious about the job. The interview process is your opportunity to conduct further research on the company and make a decision about whether or not to accept a job offer.

Listed below are sample questions that candidates may ask in a job interview. Use these as a guideline to develop your own questions. When considering what questions to ask, read over the job description and conduct company research then see what natural questions arise out of this. It is considered acceptable practice to write your questions down in advance and bring them to the job interview.

THE POSITION

1. Is this the first time your company has hired a co-op student?

2. What are the main expectations of this position?

3. What would you like done differently by the next person who fills this position?

4. What type of support does this position receive in terms of people, finances. etc?

5. What do you consider to be the main skills and qualifications that the ideal candidate for this position should possess?

6. How does this position contribute to the company's goals, productivity or profits?

7. What would be the first priority for the person who takes this position?

TRAINING/ORIENTATION

1. What type of orientation does your organization provide for co-op students?

2. Is there a training program available for all new employees?

3. How long do you anticipate the training period to be for someone taking on this role?

JOB RESPONSIBILITIES

1. What are the major responsibilities of this position?

2. What is a typical day like in the department?

3. What would be a typical first assignment?

4. What are some of the objectives you would like to see accomplished in this job? What is most pressing? What would you like to have done in the next 3 months?

5. What are some of the long term objectives you would like to see completed?

6. What are some of the more difficult problems an individual would have to face in this position? How do you think these could best be handled?

7. Would there be any opportunities to move around to various departments within your organization during a co-op placement?

8. What freedom would I have in determining my own work objectives, deadlines, and methods of measurement?

9. How current is the hardware and software that I would be expected to use, if given this position?

EVALUATION

1. How often would my performance be reviewed?

2. What type of evaluation methods does your organization utilize to review performance?

3. How does your organization recognize its employees for their contributions?

ADVANCEMENT OPPORTUNITIES

1. What advancement opportunities are available for the person who is successful in this position, and within what time frame?

2. What might the career path be for this position?

3. What can I expect in terms of job progression within the organization?

4. What accounts for success within the company?

THE ORGANIZATION

1. In terms of products and services, how has this organization been most successful over the years?

2. How would you describe the atmosphere of the organization? What is unique about it?

3. What significant changes do you foresee in the near future?

4. What would be the co-op student's most important relationships - clients, customers, other employees?

5. What are some of the departmental goals for the upcoming year?

6. Who would I be working most directly with? Who would I be reporting to? More than one person?

7. What is the background of my potential boss?

8. What are the company's long term goals?

9. What do you like best about this company? Why?

10. I've read that..... cite some company research. What are the key reasons for this success?

THE HIRING PROCESS

1. Who makes the final decision on hiring for this position?

2. Are there any questions that you have about my background that I can clarify for you?

3. Would you like a copy of my references? (Have it available to give them)

4. What is the next step in the hiring process?

5. Do you have recent graduates from McMaster University working for you?

Common Strengths

Use these words to describe your strengths, but remember to give examples. Link your strengths with specific events or actions you undertook and briefly explain how you demonstrated your skills.

- ANALYTICAL ABILITY
- MATURITY
- ABILITY TO THINK CONCEPTUALLY
- DEPENDABILITY
- ABILITY TO GET RESULTS
- FRIENDLINESS
- PRACTICAL APPROACH
- ENTHUSIASM
- HANDS ON EXPERIENCE
- CONFIDENCE
- GOOD LISTENING SKILLS
- PERSEVERANCE
- SELF -MOTIVATION
- PUNCTUALITY
- THOROUGHNESS

- SINCERITY
- COMMON SENSE
- HONESTY
- COMMUNICATION SKILLS
- ASSERTIVENESS
- WILLINGNESS TO WORK HARD
- DEDICATION
- ABILITY TO HANDLE PRESSURE
- CHARISMA
- PERSUASIVENESS
- LEADERSHIP
- ABILITY TO BE A TEAM PLAYER
- COMPETITIVENESS
- WRITING SKILLS
- ABILITY TO LEARN QUICKLY
- RESOURCEFULNESS
- PATIENCE
- SPEAKING SKILLS
- ENTREPRENEURIAL SPIRIT
- OUTGOING MANNER
- ADAPTABILITY
- ABILITY TO PAY ATTENTION TO DETAIL
- ABILITY TO SOLVE PROBLEMS

www.ingramcontent.com/pod-product-compliance
Lightning Source LLC
Chambersburg PA
CBHW070929180526
45168CB00005B/2204